Wakey-Wakey, It's Time!

Humanity, Pay Attention

Gail Alexander

PEN & PUBLISH

Saint Louis, Missouri

Published by

St. Louis, Missouri
(314) 827-6567
info@PenandPublish.com
www.PenandPublish.com

Print ISBN: 978-1-956897-71-5
e-book ISBN: 978-1-956897-72-2
Library of Congress Control Number: 2025942126

This book is printed on the USA on acid-free paper.

Dedication

Thank you to all the people I have had the privilege of creating mandalas or doing a reading/healing session with. It has been my greatest honor.

To my friends, I could not have done this without all of you.

Thank you to my mentors, teachers, and spirit team for your compassion, guidance, and grace. Thank you for supporting and encouraging me, which has helped me believe in myself as much as you have all believed in me.

To Jenniffer and Amy, thank you for believing in me and providing me with opportunities to continue growing.

To Bobbie, thank you for stepping in, guiding, and supporting me when my mother transitioned. It has meant the world to me. Love you.

To Sue, thanks for the suggestion change for the title.

To Jenn, thank you for the support, encouragement and laughter.

Preface

We are the collective that works with this one. We are a series of Arch Angels, Ascended Masters, and Light Beings. This one is capable of channeling and holding the frequency for us to all come in together instead of one a time. There is much we wish to share with humanity. The tone and cadence of this book is different than the previous books this one has authored, as the message has more of an urgency.

We thank you all for taking this journey with us. You are more capable than you know and need to remember who you are and light up this world. We come forward now to help the Earth and humanity shift into the beings you are meant to be not what you were told or instructed to be. Some of you reading this may feel us, sense us, or know we are with you as you read this book. Trust your experience. This book is intended to help humanity grow, shift, expand and illuminate. Read the questions at the end of each section and let them take you where you need to go. Sink into the mandalas/portals, and let the frequency hold you, help you and transform you.

Many blessings humanity, we are here to help.

To Humanity,

There is much love available. With that said you as humans block the magnificence of this frequency because of the power and possibility this frequency holds. Love is capable of transforming. It is time for all of you to remember the love, light and power that you all carry. It is time for you to each be who you are fully meant to be. Be your own Power Ranger, you have more support than you can fathom. Go Forth, live, laugh, love and experience connection, joy, and the beauty and gift of being incarnated. We know it does not always feel like a gift and each breath; each moment of connection is exactly that, a gift. Time to open your presents in the present. Good journey. We the collective are always here for you, sending peace, grace, blessings and love.

—The Collective

Contents

Foreword

Once again, Gail Alexander, with *Wakey-Wakey, It's Time! Humanity, Pay Attention*, has written another book that holds loving space for you to realize exactly how beautiful and cherished you are. In this book, Gail shares stories of how she has become comfortable with her cosmic awareness so you can do the same. It is time for us to remember we are one divine soul here to discover the magnificent light each fractal of our soul has to offer one another as we create an unimaginably wondrous cosmic light symphony.

This book offers portals of loving cosmic wisdom that gently guide you to play Wake Up. These portals come in Gail's Mandalas, stories, exploratory questions, meditations, and the loving heart she shares to soften your limbic system into surrendering to your magnificence. As Gail says, it is time to remember, "We are each a lighthouse" and all of our lighthouses are essential to creation.

As Gail guides you to love yourself and your light, you will realize that the only path to discovering the magnificence of God/the Universe/Source/the Divine lies within you. The book guides you to have the strength and courage to be who you are meant to be without the need for external validation from others and even to be comfortable with the idea that "what other people think of you is none of your business."

I have been blessed to know Gail for less than two years, and in this short amount of time, she has helped me in innumerable ways to remember the divine fractal of our being that my human suit is yearning to share in this dimension. She helped me embody a frequency of confidence through knowing, believing in, and then surrendering in the felt sense to the gifts I have to share. She also helped me heal so many of my "not enoughs" that I am now actively choosing not to "play small" with my gifts.

Her guidance and wisdom have helped me surrender to channeling wisdom instead of knowledge and walk in the frequency of the "who" I will manifest today. When we find the freedom and the confidence to create an infinite channel of who we are meant to be in the now and do not stay confined to the box of ego energy we have previously imagined ourselves to be, there is no better way to play creation.

We are all channels of a unique fractal of divine wisdom(love). This wisdom is not knowledge. It is not a blueprint, idea, concept, or teachable through the limited vibration of words. It is the opening and embodying of the unique stream of universal heart coherence your soul fractal is meant to glow with. It is the bliss of connecting to glowing fractals of the entirety of our soul through the surrender to the glow of the light within you.

When our soul fractals glow in unison through the power of a humble, surrendered pride in our perceived individual light, we will create an earth dimension that is beautiful beyond our wildest dreams. Even better yet, we will wake up to a frequency of love where we realize we are already creating a beautiful earth. Gail will help you wake up to the wisdom that you have labeled as pain and suffering and will lead you to search for the love that reignites the fractal of light of y/our soul.

Thank you, Gail, for your endless desire to teach humanity how to love itself, and your dedication to loving the earth, which creates this precious dimension for us to play creation in. Also, thank you for all the mandalas (portals of wisdom) you have drawn to help me remember how beautiful and fun it is to play creation with our soul.

Julie Foster, MD

Author of *Remembering Awake: How to Love and Play Creation with Y/our Soul*

Introduction

Have you ever thought you were meant to do something but had no idea what or how you would do it? If you have read any of my previous books, you know I often get these hunches or ideas. This book is no different. I could not get the title out of my head. My spirit team is pushing me to write this; why? Because it is time, that's why. *Wakey-Wakey It's Time! Humanity, Pay Attention.*

We need to wake up and realize there is more to being human, alive and awake, than we think or have been led to believe. This is the time we have all waited for. This is when we can shift humanity's consciousness to create the world of peace, hope, and love we envision for ourselves and leave behind the world of fear, hate, and divisiveness.

Sitting in front of my computer typing, I keep hearing *wakey-wakey*. It is a message I have heard since 2020. In my book *The Great Awakening of 2020: A Mandalic Journey*, one of the mandalas I drew was called *Wakey-Wakey*. That was the beginning of humanity's need to wake up.

We are at a significant turning point, and we all have our own part to play. We are each a lighthouse. Who do you want to share your light with? How do you want to spread your light? What is your purpose? What is your path? What are you meant to do? How are you going to do it? We are all facing these questions right now.

My spirit team does not want to instill fear, just the importance of being and living in the present moment. This is the only space in which we can affect change. Wakey, Wakey. Let's go. We have got this; we just have to believe that we do.

We are not seeing the signs the Earth is trying to show us that we work and live in tandem. Humans cannot do whatever we want on the planet and think there will be no repercussions. There is usually a cause-and-effect relationship, and it is time to start to look at what we are causing and how the planet is reacting.

It is time for humanity to think about something other than our own selfish needs and start to look at the symbiotic relationship between humans, the planet, and all other living beings. Everything has an energy. We have turned our backs on the ancient wisdom of Aborigines, Native Americans, Shamans, Elders, etc. There are messages the human race needs to start paying attention to, or we will no longer exist. Spirit wants to work with us to help us, as well as help us evolve. Other forces do not wish for humanity's evolution and increasing awareness. After all, the third Dimension is all about polarities.

This is the third Dimension: good versus evil, love versus hate.

We are in an endless loop. For those who remember answering machines with the tape, that is what we do as humans. We keep doing the same things, expecting different outcomes. I am sorry, but that is the definition of insanity. Yet, here we are again as a consciousness, trying to decide what we will do and be.

As humanity, we cannot continue to use the same solutions we have always used because those are just band-aids. We don't need a quick fix. We need a transformation. What are we going to do? I am on the edge of my seat to discover what choice our consciousness makes. Once the choice has been made, we are all ready to get to work and help with the transition and transformation.

This book is filled with information and suggestions on how to work through things. There will be questions after each section for you to ask yourself to move forward. I look forward to taking this journey with each and every one of you. If we work together and believe change is possible, then it is. Our beliefs create our reality. Again, what do you want to create? What and who do you want to be? What do you want to put out into the world? Now is the time to decide. It is imperative.

It's go time. The very future of humanity depends on us. We are the ones we have been waiting for. We are the ones who need to be the change-makers and light-bringers.

Are you ready?

So, as I like to say in all my books:

Buckle up, keep your arms and legs in the vehicle until it stops completely, and away we go.

Section One:

Preparation

Message from the Collective

We are the collective working with this one to bring this information to humanity. We are Angels, Ascended Masters, Light Beings, and Arch Angels. This book is different; it is being written in collaboration with the other side.

It is time for humanity to live from the heart space, not the head space. You are safe to explore your gifts and abilities. We are shielding those brave enough to do this work.

We want humanity to hear, feel, and see our message. We wish to help all of you who are willing and brave enough to do the work and transform the human race. This is not a race; this is a way of being. There is no prize at the end of this "race," only love and soul growth. Take this journey with us. We will help illuminate your path or introduce you to others who can illuminate your path.

Have you ever felt guided or pulled to work with someone and talked yourself out of it? That was us helping to guide you. However, that pesky free will gets in the way sometimes.

Trust the hunches, the knowingness, the feelings. Energy does not lie; other people and thoughts often do.

You need to bypass your ego, as this stops you. Sometimes, the journey is not linear; sometimes, it feels chaotic, and sometimes, it feels like you can't go on. Trust us, you can and will go on. You are never done growing as a human being until you take your last breath in your human suit. Then, your soul continues to journey.

We are here, witnessing and supporting you humans in your freedom from oppression. Take our hands and walk with us. Let us help you. Together, we can truly free humanity if that is what the majority of human consciousness wants.

We are putting a quote in this one's head that she has said before, as that is how we wish to end here.

—The Collective

Quote:

"When you come to the edge of all that you know, you must believe one of two things: Either there will be ground to stand on, or you will be given wings to fly."

—O. R. Melling

Realizations and Awarenesses

Signs are all around you when you are present, messages to help you make decisions, and messages about which direction to go.

Most of us are oblivious, and some forces of the Earth want us to stay asleep and not pay attention. Like Lemmings that just follow the crowd and the mind-think of the crowd instead of thinking for ourselves.

However, if you become mindful and open yourself up enough, and connect to yourself and your internal GPS system, there is guidance everywhere. For example, some people see license plates with messages for them, some see feathers or loose change, and some hear the perfect song. Other ways can be getting a phone call and knowing who it is before you look at the caller ID. Sometimes, you suddenly get chills or know you are not alone, even when you are physically alone. Sometimes your plans change, or you are running late, and you don't know why, then you hear there was an accident or event you were not meant to be involved in. These are all signs that information beyond our five senses is always coming in.

In this book, I will discuss different examples in my life where I received signs and messages, knew something was going to happen, or felt uneasy. These are the kinds of things we need to pay attention to.

There is a reason I joke that my life is a science fiction movie and always has been: the number of experiences I have had allude to this. The difference is that I do not think I am different from any other human being, only that I pay attention. So, this book will help you learn how to pay attention to the signs and messages around you and start to process that information.

I have written several books on this topic already, but they (my Spirit team) want me to discuss it and explain it differently in this book.

I am very fortunate to know several of my gifts, and I have been honored and privileged to help others connect with theirs. We all have gifts and abilities and, for whatever reason, do not feel comfortable using them. It may be messages from others, beliefs, judgment, fear, not being believed, or they were so strong that we didn't know what to do with them. Most of us have had lifetimes where we were killed for using our gifts and speaking our truth, which might explain why so many people are sluggish to fully embrace their gifts now.

My journey to use my gifts and abilities has spanned my entire life. Like so many before me, I shut them off for a long time, and then they returned, which is what some of my other books are about. They chronicle this journey of reawakening

One of the ways my spirit team communicates with me is through song lyrics and choruses. One of the songs they sing often is "Spinning Wheels" by Blood Sweat and Tears. I heard it again while parking my car in the garage right before writing this section. I just started laughing because I was trying to get home to work on this book after lunch which ended up being longer than anticipated. They were letting me know it was time to start working. Also, on my way to lunch I saw the license plate *Hes Risn*. I said to myself, thanks for being with me today, Jesus. Jesus started laughing.

This is the time humanity has been waiting for—for humans to take their place in the universe and rediscover what the human suit and your light body blended together can do. As a consciousness, we have all been told what it can and cannot do, and then there is the truth about what it can actually do.

We have been weighed down. We have all bought into the idea that being human means there are limitations. This is not correct.

There are no limitations. Only what we believe is a limitation. Then we go about setting it up for ourselves.

At times, brilliance shines through, but we forget to recognize and celebrate it. Some of us have read about ancient civilizations and what they could do, and then that technology or knowledge is lost because humanity pushed too far. This will be discussed further in an upcoming section.

We are at that time again. What do we want to create as a human consciousness? Do we still have a moral compass?

We are a very egocentric race of beings and have been more cerebral at times. Now, the time is upon us to open our hearts and balance the heart, mind, body, soul, and light together. We can do this; many have done it before, and many will do it after.

Why not us, and why not now? That is the question I always come back to. Why not us? Why can we not fully open up and be who we are meant to be? Why not now? What are we waiting for?

Sometimes, we get bogged down in waiting for signs or waiting for the universe to speak to us through guides, signs, music, etc. What if they are doing all those things and we are still not paying attention? What if you get the sign? Then you question everything about it, not trusting it or believing it. How much do you think your lack of trust and belief is going to affect your journey and the information you could still receive?

Makes me think of the story of a man in a flood praying to God to save him. A boat comes by to rescue him and he says no, thank you. I am waiting for God to save me. The water gets higher, and he is on his roof. A helicopter comes to help him and the man says no, he is waiting for God to help him. The man drowns and goes to heaven and asks God why he didn't save him. God replied: who do you think sent the boat and the helicopter?

I told this famous story because we envision our signs coming in a specific way, and that is not always how they come. Sometimes you hear the same thing multiple times from people and you write it off as a coincidence. Is it, though? Be open to things you hear, see, feel, and know. Trust your hunches.

Ultimately, the question becomes, how do you start to trust yourself, your knowledge, your intuition, and your internal guidance and block out the rest? This is what we are going to address in this book: how to tune into yourself, how to pay attention, and how to get the answers you are desperately searching for.

Questions:

What signs are you waiting for?

How do you start to open up?

How do you begin to trust?

Let's Start at the Very Beginning

I was talking with a friend about writing this book and being blocked. My spirit team always has a sense of humor and a penchant for music, as I mentioned. So they shared a song from *The Sound of Music,* "Let's Start at the Very Beginning."

So, that is what I am going to do. I am starting at the very beginning. The beginning for me is sharing how this book came to be. I wanted to put together a compilation book with chapters from multiple people.

My spirit team again laughing, saying:

"No, that may come later, you need to write a whole book on this topic yourself because it is what you do. You help people awaken to their authentic selves, which is part of why you are on the planet right now. You hold so much wisdom and knowledge about and around humanity. You have the ability to recall past lives; you work with the Earth and with crystals. You, my dear, are a record keeper of the Earth, and you have agreed to come back at this time to help humanity once again."

Wow, that was so succinct and took me by surprise. Usually, when I ask what my purpose is and why I am here, they do not answer. So, this was very interesting to read back.

As with most humans, I sometimes doubt the information I am getting. Sometimes, even after everything I have seen and experienced, I am still skeptical. When I say that to other people they get really discouraged and say, "If you still think that with all you can do, what chance do I have?"

The human condition is where we have skepticism and sometimes don't trust. Did you ever think that was part of what we are meant to overcome to break free of the forces controlling the Earth? We have been controlled for eons because of our skepticism, doubt, and fear. The only real truth is peace, love, and light; everything else was created to keep us playing small.

It is so interesting when you think about this and what it all means. I often start questioning myself as to why I need to be here again. I know what my spirit team just told me above, and I still question it. I remember a past life in Egypt when I got angry at humanity for making what I deemed "stupid" decisions and not wanting to move forward. I reacted out of anger, which was not a good outcome for the people in Egypt.

We have all had lifetimes where we have done things we wished we hadn't, and even in our current lifetime, many of us have regrets. My friend Dr. Julie Foster always says there is really only one of us here. Think about that for a moment. If there is really only one of us here, then your decisions affect the whole of humanity and the path of humanity. Mind-blowing, I know. It is time to move out of ego, as the collective mentioned at the beginning of this book.

My whole life, I have felt different. I never belonged. I never fit in. I saw the world differently than everyone else. No one quite knew what to do with me or how to nurture this gift. I went into detail about this in my first book, *I Don't Know How I Know, I Just Know*. Suffice it to say, that I had to shut off everything I knew in order to grow up and survive my childhood. I know I am not the only one who has had this experience. How many others reading this had to shut things down at different parts of their lives to survive? Think about how many people struggle with addictions of all kinds because life is painful, and people are constantly trying to escape the pain of being human and having human experiences.

The lesson in all of this is that we need to lean into the pain, not to relive all of it, but to free it from our bodies and the auric field.

What if that is the lesson in being human? Not numbing pain, but transforming it into our greatest strength. We have all had pain, and that is partly what has connected so many of us. What if the lesson in moving to the fifth Dimension isn't one of pain? What if it is one of love? What if loving yourself is what it is going to take to free yourself and for us to free humanity?

It is a hard concept to understand and an even harder concept to wrap our human brains around. Yet, this is the truth. Pain and suffering are keeping us stuck in an endless loop. It is how we have been conditioned to behave and function. However, it no longer needs to stay this way. We can break the karmic pattern and evolve.

Think about all the horrific things that have happened and continue to happen on Earth. Then, think about the human Spirit and how it can transcend everything. I believe this is the message for moving into the fifth Dimension and living from our hearts. By living from our hearts, we will all have deeper connections with ourselves and our Spirit and soul. I believe this is where humanity needs to move if we are going to continue to be inhabitants of the Earth. The Earth is changing, and now it is our turn to change.

These can be really difficult concepts to take in. On some level, though, you can feel the truth of these words and what it brings up for you.

Questions:

Where can you start to love yourself?

Can you see how your path intersects and weaves into other's paths?

What do you want the impact of your life to mean?

What do you believe in?

Growing Up

When I was younger, I am not going to say little, because I do not think that is accurate . . . so, when I was a child I had just as much wisdom and knowing as I do now which made it very challenging for my family.

I remember sitting in the car while my mother was driving, thinking: Why are we here? What is the purpose of Earth? Why are so many people unhappy? How do we change things? Not what a 5- or 6-year-old typically ponders.

I was trying to understand why we as human beings chose the things we did and why we continue to make similar choices. I started wondering what the learning curve is for humanity. We do not seem to evolve too quickly. If you look at history and how it has played out, humanity seems to like to stay stuck and go around in circles.

Growing up, I had a white pedal car, and that is how I thought I traveled multi-dimensionally. One of the neighborhood kids always took my white pedal car, and I would be so scared because he didn't know how to travel multi-dimensionally. My parents would always get my car back, and I would feel relieved and safe again. As I got older, I realized that it was not the car that allowed me to travel multi-dimensionally. It was me. I still travel multi-dimensionally all the time. I am fortunate that I can pull from many dimensions to help humanity shift.

I also grew up Jewish in this lifetime and remember sitting in the Synagogue thinking it was so strange that we had to go through someone else, in this case, the Rabbi, to connect to G-d. I connected to G-d all the time, so again, I thought it was strange and did not understand why the grown-ups around me did not understand these basic things. I still do not understand how my fellow grown-ups do not understand these things. It seems as plain as day. Therefore, I thought everyone saw the world the same way I did. I have discovered that is not the case.

When I was 12, I was sent to an overnight camp. This was the first time I remember having the experience of bilocating. I remember standing in the canteen at the camp, and the next thing I knew, I was home at my house playing with my friends. Then someone called my name and I was yanked back into my body at camp. It was the weirdest experience, and I did not have anyone to talk to about it. I was like, what just happened? I was scared that it was going to happen again because it was not planned. I was not in meditation or trying to bilocate, it just happened. I wish I had someone I could have talked to about all the things that happened while I was growing up, but it freaked out all the adults around me.

If anyone saw the *X-Men* movies where the mutants all lit up on a grid so they knew where to find them, that's how I see humanity. I see the grid we all create and that we are all just a point of light on this grid. We are the ones lighting up the world. We still have not fully realized what can happen, what can shift, if enough of us band together.

I want to normalize these experiences for people. We are not crazy, we just see, feel and experience the world differently. These were things I tried to hide, and now they are things I want to share with everyone. Perspective is such an interesting thing, the events do not change, just the way we see the world or the event that changes.

Questions:

Have you ever felt different?

Have you ever felt like you do not belong?

Do you see the world differently and don't understand why others don't see the world that way?

Signs and Messages: Cars and Planes

I had to take my Jeep in for service as there was a leak. The dealership said a new gasket was needed to stop the leak. So, as I sat there waiting for them to change it out, I kept hearing that I was not to get back in that Jeep. The gasket was not the problem. Keep in mind that I had that Jeep for less than two years. I pushed the thought away because I knew what I still owed on it and did not see how I could do anything different. Again, getting direct guidance and not fully trusting it? Does anyone else ever feel that?

After 45 minutes they said my Jeep was done and I could drive it home. I knew it was not fixed, I just had this hunch and intuition. I felt uneasy. When I got into my Jeep there was an offer as to what they would give me for that Jeep. I thought that was interesting, because I had not expressed any interest in trading it in. I love how subtle or not-so-subtle my spirit team is sometimes.

So, when I got home, I went upstairs, got a piece of cardboard, went back to the garage I parked in, and put it under my Jeep. About two hours later, when I was done with my meetings for work, I went back downstairs and, sure enough, the Jeep was still leaking. I drove back to the dealership, where they tried to tell me that it was just extra runoff. I looked at the technician working on my Jeep and asked if he had checked all the seals. This time, they gave me a rental car.

This is not the first time I have had this experience with a vehicle. My previous Jeep had something moving every time I turned. I kept taking it back to the dealership, and I told them there was something under my seat that was loose and moved every time I turned. Instead, they checked the steering, the brakes, everything. I really was beginning to think I was going crazy, and they just wrote me off as a crazy female who didn't know what she was talking about. After six months, they finally found the four-inch bold under the driver's seat was the culprit.

Trusting your intuition is important. Needless to say, I was right the whole time; I just knew what the issue was, but they needed to do it their way. I lot of wasted time. They broke my power seat when they took it out to get the bolt. So, I got to spend even more time at the dealership. Yeah (said very sarcastically). Sorry, I digressed there for a moment. I'm back to the current Jeep story.

The next day I called and followed up with the dealership and they said the seal was cracked on the oil plate and being the state of the world we currently are living in was going to take over a week to get the part and fix it. I still had this gnawing feeling that there was something else going on that they were not even looking at. I asked to be connected to one of the salesman.

As it turns out, I was given to one of the best salesmen, so after work I went in and test-drove a Jeep and received an offer within 45 minutes. The offer was a little bit more than I wanted to pay, so I asked if I could think about it and get back to them tomorrow. They said fine, as I had bought several cars from their dealership in the past. That night I was looking online, and there was a very similar Jeep, a little less expensive. I reached out to the salesman and said this is what I want my payments to be. I got a call back and he said done; come get your new Jeep.

Usually, you are in the dealership for hours, and they wear you down. I knew this was divinely guided by the way it was working out. So I said thank you, Spirit Team. On the way to the dealership, I was still struggling with the cost and having some doubts as people around me believed that I was doing the wrong thing. I am still human. My mother's best friend called me out of the blue, and we were talking. I was telling her about my doubts, and she said to buy the new Jeep. You deserve it. I am crying as I type this. I looked up and said thank you, Mom. I know my mom in heaven got her friend to call me to deliver the exact message that I needed to hear. Then, all the doubts disappeared. I walked in, the Jeep was full of gas and detailed. They handed me the keys to test drive this one and when I came back, I signed some papers with the salesman, and transferred my belongings. There were a lot as I had no idea I was getting a new vehicle. Then I went and signed the financial paperwork and left within 45 minutes. That was quite something.

Of course, a few weeks later all the tariffs in the United States started to hit so I got it at the perfect time. Again, I said thank you spirit team.

My reason for sharing this with all of you is that when you trust and follow your intuition, things have a way of working out for your highest good. Often times when something is right, and guided, it turns out to be very synchronistic and everything just flows.

This has been coming up a lot recently, so I am going to share it with all of you. Your vehicle is an extension of yourself. Besides your body, it is the vehicle that gets you around from place to place. The names of my vehicles have always meant something to me, so I am going to go through some of them with you here because I think it is an important and interesting way to gather some information about yourself.

My first ever vehicle when I was 16 was an Eagle, which is interesting when you think about it because I was learning to spread my wings and fly.

I had a Pontiac Grand Prix special touring edition. I did so much driving when I had those vehicles it is really funny. Also I tend to like to drive a little faster than the speed limit, but don't tell anyone. Seems to be something all the women in my family did.

Here is where it starts to get interesting. I had a Pontiac Aztek, and with that vehicle, I had three spirit passengers who sat in my back seat and went with me everywhere I went. It was two males and a female. They were just always there. They would not talk often, they would smile and enjoy the selection of music that was played. They were always just looking out the windows and taking it all in. It was just so interesting. When my lease was up, I got a Pontiac vibe, kind of pressured into that one, and it never felt right. I didn't have that car for very long. The Vibe had a bad vibe for me.

Then I moved to Saturn and had a couple SUVs called Vue's. One of the Vue's I had was bright lime green. I had an accident in that vehicle and was injured and had to have surgery. While I was in the deposition my lawyer finally saw the color of the vehicle in a photo and said how do you miss that?

Then I had a Jeep Compass and this is when my gifts were starting to come back so it made a lot of sense. I then moved to an Escape and this is when my mother got diagnosed with cancer and things were sad and difficult. I traded that in for a Jeep Renegade after she died as that was how I was feeling, I was rebellious, sad, angry and a renegade. Then I just moved back to a Compass because I am now the compass showing the path to others.

There are signs everywhere if we start to pay attention to them.

We make choices all the time that we are not aware of. These are just some interesting things to think about.

Moving on to some experiences I have had with planes and intuition and getting signs. I was sitting in the airport waiting for my flight and just kept having this odd sense that there was something wrong with the plane. I couldn't shake it no matter how much I tried to distract myself and reassure myself that everything was going to be okay, because deep down I did not believe that it was going to be.

As I sat there, I started to go within and meditate and asked to illuminate the plane to reveal the issue so that the airline would see it before we got on the plane. I do not know how long I was sitting there, but I jerked back into my body, hearing that my flight was moving to a different gate and a new plane. There was a mechanical issue that could not be fixed before the scheduled flight. I was so grateful that I did not have to get on that plane. When I got to the new gate with the new plane, I checked in and heard that everything was going to be okay.

Sometimes, it is important to trust your intuition to do what you can. I don't know if I would have gotten on the plane if it had not been changed. Learning to trust our own internal wisdom, those hunches we all get from our intuition, can take time, because some of us were raised to not trust it. Think about messages you grew up receiving around intuition, imaginary friends, and Spirit, and how that is playing a role in your life now.

Another plane experience and trusting your intuition was the time I was on a flight with my mom and grandmother. The pilot was having trouble getting one of the engines started. We were all on the plane, and they were not letting anyone off. This was before I had reopened all my gifts. Everyone on the plane was anxious and scared. You could cut the tension. I somehow knew we were going to be okay and that nothing was going to happen. We took off and I will say everyone held their breath through the whole flight, but we made it safely.

These are just two examples of how our intuition is always there if we choose to listen.

Questions:

Have you ever thought about the name of your vehicle and what that could mean for you?

Have you ever thought about why you chose the color of your vehicle and what that means?

Have you ever had a feeling before getting on a flight that something was going to happen, or had the airline change the plane you were supposed to fly out on?

Numbers

While trying to figure out what else I was writing about in this book, of course, the collective and my spirit team jumped in. The day before writing this section, I saw many angel numbers on the clock whenever I looked up. I saw 9:11, which was really interesting to me today, and that was a signal to me that something important was going to happen. As it turns out, the morning that I saw 9 1 1 was the day that I channeled all the messages for this book from the collective. 9 1 1 also makes me think of the Twin Towers and how so much of the world came together over that event. Why is it always a tragedy that unites us? Why can't it be joy and love? Again, this is a choice.

On some days I see all the Angel numbers and I always think how special this day is going to be and then thank the angels for the winks and support. 11:11 12:12, 1:11, 2:22 and 3:33, 4:44.

It is unusual for me to see 5:55 as I am no longer at work and not really paying attention to the time. However, clearly, I was working on this book. After work, my head jerked up to see it was 5:55. Then, in my dreamtime that night, I kept seeing signs like the speed limit signs of 55. So interesting how they get messages to us so that we pay attention. Often, they will repeat it over and over until you get the message. The other number I see every day, usually twice a day, is 8:23, which was my mother's human birthday, and I just stop whatever I am doing and say hi, Mom.

The sequence of numbers is important to pay attention to, as well, to determine what they mean to you. Of course look them up, there are so many different sites you can do that on or just google the number.

Lately, I have been seeing 411. When I was growing up in the dark ages before cell phones and the internet, when you needed information or an address or phone number, you dialed 4 1 1 on your landline phone and then talked to an operator, a real person, not AI. Every time I see 4 1 1, I think about what information I am going to get or what I need, and it brings a smile to my face. When I was growing up we got to talk to actual live people. Now you just ask your phone and the information is instantaneous. I am fearful that we are losing our ability to think for ourselves and no longer know how to have conversations with people unless we are texting.

Questions:

Do numbers hold any significance for you?

Do you see certain repeating numbers?

Section Two:

Integration

Message to Humanity

The time is upon you to make a choice. What direction do you want to go? What do you want for yourselves as individuals and as a consciousness? There has never been a more important time than now.

As the Earth moves into the Fifth Dimension, you personally have a choice as to what direction you wish to go. This may be the end-of-the-earth adventure game for you if you choose not to awaken. Just like in the times of Jesus, the message for our time is love, grace, flow, balance, and being in the present moment. It is time to remember and realize you have the power within. You get to choose.

You are not a lemming (video game where the lemmings all follow each other no matter what their fate). That is what you have been conditioned to believe. That is not what and who humanity is. Humans are light beings who have lost their way due to the control of other forces on Earth. This is the time for humanity and consciousness to break free, and for each of us to take our place, realizing that we all have an infinite power and light within us. We have just forgotten how to connect to it. Now is the time. Are you with the forces of change, or do you want to get left in the dust?

—The Collective

Guidance from Ascended Master Jesus

Jesus was about compassion and love, those were his original messages. The messages were not about control. Men twisted these messages to control humanity and changed a lot of the original teachings for this purpose. When you become more aware, conscious, and you trust your intuition, you can see how some messages are used to manipulate human beings for the purposes of the beings in control.

We are seeing this play out across the world right now. There is still time to change the trajectory, and it is going to take a majority of us to wake up and be willing to fight for our freedom. Humans no longer need to be controlled, it is important that we remember who we really are, why we are really here, and what we are really capable of.

In my book *I Don't Know How I Know ... I Just Know,* I channeled a series of messages from Jesus and called them the Jesus Blessings. I am going to list some of them here for you as well. They are important messages for humanity to really think about and connect with.

- May you have faith in yourself and your gifts.
- May you find peace, acceptance, and clarity in yourself and your life.
- May you use your voice and stand up for what you believe in.
- May you believe you can make a difference—because you can.
- May you have the strength and courage to be who you are meant to be regardless of what others think, do or say.
- May you connect and live through your heart.

- May you follow your bliss and your path.
- May you learn to bend, flex, and live in the flow.
- May you fully accept and love yourself as you are – a divine spark.
- May you be true to yourself.
- May you be full of joy, laughter, spontaneity and awe.
- May you be in peace and grace.
- May you be able to receive that which is present for you.
- May you be awake and make conscious choices.
- May you have the power to live fully in the moment.
- May you be able to count your blessings.
- May you know how loved and cared for you truly are every minute of every day, because you are.
- May you always be true to yourself and dance to the beat of your soul.

Questions:

Are you ready to be free?

Are you ready to be the light being you are in a human suit?

Spiritual Development

They want me to share a couple of experiences I have had while doing some work on myself. I had a family constellation therapy Session with Julie Grant, and at the end of the session, I saw golden light connecting the whole Earth through a grid of golden light. It was like someone flipped on a light switch. It was so powerful and peaceful at the same time. The Christos light is flooding the Earth again to help us on our path. It was one of the most amazing things I have seen. Power, peace and light balanced. I will admit that I have checked several times since then to make sure it is still flowing and continues to flow.

A few days later I was in my class with Heather Sprigg where we did a healing meditation. The golden light vision from above continued in this experience. I was shown a pyramid that felt Aztekian or Mayan. It was not the shape of the pyramids of Egypt. I was encouraged to walk up the steps of this pyramid, and as I started climbing the steps, there was a 24-karat gold lion on either side of me walking up the steps all the way to the top.

As we walked up the steps, we brought the golden light that had been ignited a few days ago up the pyramid one step at a time until it shot out the top of the pyramid and covered the Earth in a golden dome. The golden Lions still appear to me to let me know they are now guarding the golden light and it will not be extinguished again. It is very comforting to know. Just to be clear, they were real, 24-karat gold lions, not statues that were moving.

The difference between this book and the last book is that there are other masters, teachers, and loved ones working with me this time, not just Metatron. It has taken me a while to adjust to the different energies in this book.

So, being who I am, I immediately went and looked up what golden lions and 24-karat golden lions mean. I was really intrigued by something I found that stated a golden lion represents wisdom, prosperity and divine authority. Golden lions also symbolize enlightenment and the pursuit of knowledge. I thought to myself that it was really cool, as that is exactly how the session and meditation felt.

Some of the other meanings I came across: golden lions can symbolize strength, courage, leadership, nobility, signs of new opportunities and success, and can be associated with the sun. Again, that all made total sense to me.

Questions:

What are some symbols, animals, or messages you receive when you meditate?

Are you able to take in the information, or do you write it off?

Ideas

We are here at this time on Earth to bring in the light. It is really that simple. We are the ones we are waiting for. We are the light bringers. It is time to fully be yourself. Do not play small. We are here to illuminate the possibilities of what Earth has for each of us and what Earth was designed to do. War and hate were not what Earth was created for. Earth is a hub for many dimensions, galaxies and beings. In some ways, we are the center, and so many watch us to see how we are navigating the human suit.

Suffice it to say that we are not doing so well in the navigation department; we are literally going backward and not forward. Sometimes, the past has a way of resurfacing to see if that is the direction we really want to go in again.

I, for one, do not want to go backward. I have been on Earth many lifetimes to help humanity rise above, and we have the potential to do that in this lifetime. I am ready to help, as are others, when humans make choices aligned with this goal.

Right now, it is just a game of hurry up and wait. It looks like humans are going to move forward, and then they are like, no, too scary, don't want to do that. Those of us who are here to help with raising the consciousness of humanity and the Earth just want to move forward, complete our missions, and help humanity see its true potential.

Wakey-Wakey is just a reminder that the time is upon us. Let's go. We know what the past shows and what happens, so let's see what the present and the future of humanity is if we move forward. Aren't you the least bit curious of what the true potential is?

To be honest, I have been shown many possibilities of what humanities choices could be. Some are more positive than others. You get a vote. What do you want? Start being, living and spreading the light you carry with others. Be the beacon, be the hope, hold the faith.

I am going to use my favorite example from *The Little Book of Eating Disorder Wisdom*, which I coauthored. We are all in the Wonkavator from the original Willy Wonka movie, and we have pressed every button but one. We have gone sideways, byways, diagonal ways, forward and back. We have never gone straight up and out. It is time. We need to crash through the glass ceiling so we can have a new 365-degree view of what is possible. Let's do it! Let's crash the glass ceiling and shift human consciousness; it is within our scope and possibility to do this.

Questions:

When you tap into humanity, what impressions or feelings do you get?

Are you staying connected and grounded during these times of transition?

Spiritual Practice

One of the things the collective that is channeling this book has asked me to talk about is spiritual practice. What is yours? How do you connect? How do you go inward, as that is where the truth and all the answers lie? Are you willing to tap in and go there? The rest is just outside noise to keep us distracted and prevent us from fulfilling what we came here to do while keeping those in power who are benefitting from all the chaos.

What is your truth? Are you fully living and embracing your truth? These are questions you need to start answering for yourself instead of focusing on what you have been taught to believe. What is important is not what your religious affiliation is or what the group thinks. Instead . . . what do you believe? What do you want to live your life by?

What is your credo for life? This is an assignment I used to give to my clients when I was a practicing therapist. If you do not have a belief system, then what are you working towards?

I am sharing two different ways to help you decipher the principles you live your life by. Take out a piece of paper or pull up a blank document on your computer and either write or type the word LIFE and see what comes up. Then, get another piece of blank paper or blank document on your computer and write or type CREED to LIVE BY and see what comes through.

Life

Life is about living in the present moment.

Life is about being kind and treating myself and others with compassion.

Life is about laughter, joy, and having fun.

Life is about love, accepting and giving it.

Life is about perspective and what filter you choose to see it through.

Life is about friendships, people, and places that enhance your life.

Life is about going inward, finding your own GPS system, and trusting it.

Life is about connecting and realizing everything has a vibration and frequency.

Creed to Live by:

Take each day as it comes.

Take time to play, to laugh and have fun every day.

Don't take yourself or life too seriously.

Breathe in and out every day and connect with yourself.

Take time to just be present in the moment.

Place your own oxygen mask on first before assisting others. In other words take time for yourself and make sure your cup runneth over before trying to help others.

Be silly.

Live in peace and grace.

Connect and live through your heart.

Be the person you want to be out in the world.

What other people think of you is none of your business.

Learn to trust your own intuition.

Fight for what you believe in.

Use your voice and learn to be in your own power.

Life is short—what are you waiting for?

Be fully alive and connect.

When you get hurt, realize you are living, and it is a natural human emotion—do not shut down!

Learn to center yourself.

Accept and love yourself for who you already are, but continue to grow, change, and develop.

Life is a journey, not a destination.

Keep moving forward.

Don't let fear stand in your way.

Be in your full power, and don't let anyone take that away from you.

Be kind and gentle with yourself and others.

Be the light you are, and let it shine for others to see.

Just be you. That is enough.

Here's an interesting thing. If you go back to the guidance section, you'll find these examples are very similar to the Jesus Blessings that were channeled. We are all connected, we are all here to raise consciousness and have a spiritual connection while in the human suit.

Questions:

What was this process like for you?

Did this help you connect to some of your core principles?

What did it feel like when you read them to yourself?

Relationships

Relationships in our human lives come and go. Sometimes we think people who are going to be with us our entire lifetime are only with us for a season. Sometimes people we think will only be in our lives for a short time are there for our entire life. Going back to what Dr. Julie Foster talked about, there is really only one of us here. With that said, we are mirrors for each other, showing us all areas we still need to grow and experience.

In relationships, when something causes a strong reaction in you, how do you work through that? The issue is presenting itself to you to give you an opportunity to grow and move forward. Are you going to take the opportunity? There is no right or wrong here; it is about human and soul growth development.

Relationships change for a variety of reasons. Sometimes, the person has fulfilled what they are meant to teach you or to learn from you. They have played their role, and it is time to exit stage left. Sometimes, we need to let go of people because the relationships are detrimental or hurtful to our human experience.

I have to say, this is a really difficult thing to do. I have had to let go of two very close friends. One transitioned, which was even more difficult because of how things were left. The other one who I thought would be a part of my life until my dying days was toxic and sucked out my life force. I had to choose between the friendship and myself. Luckily, I chose myself. That was not always the case for me.

Coming to Earth this lifetime, I know that my path is one of service. I have always known that from a very young age, while also knowing that sometimes I did not choose myself. I thought that helping the other person was what I needed to do to fulfill my mission. As I age in human years, I realize what I have often said in my books is true. We have to put on our own oxygen mask first before assisting others. This analogy has always stuck with me. The truth seems to stick.

Think about relationships in your own life. Have you hung on long after you knew it was over out of a sense of obligation, dependency, fear? Sometimes it is really hard to put yourself first and yet that is what we need to do. We are all human beings, not human doings, and we need time for ourselves to recharge, re-energize, and revitalize. Sometimes it is okay to have alone time.

Our soul is having an experience in the human suit and we have made agreements with other souls before we return as to what role we need them to play and what we want to work on. Relationships are ways for our soul to grow, evolve, and love.

Sometimes, the healthiest thing is to let go, even if it doesn't feel good. We are not here to sacrifice ourselves. That role has already been taken. We are here to love, evolve, grow, and learn lessons. How you learn is up to you.

This is where the conversation of free will always comes in. If everything has been decided before we returned, how do we have free will? My answer and the answer my spirit team has given me is that free will comes in with how we choose to handle all the things we agreed too and how long it takes for us to handle them. Relationships are one of the fastest ways to learn, grow and evolve.

As a therapist, I spent a lot of time talking with clients I worked with about the differences between loneliness, isolation, and being alone. Sometimes, we need time by ourselves. To be alone. Isolating and feeling lonely are not the same thing because feelings of sadness and worthlessness can come up. At the same time, being alone is something you have chosen to do to support your spiritual practice and healing. We need connection in the human suit and need support, love, compassion, and encouragement. With that said, sometimes you also need to be your own cheerleader and be proud of things you have done and accomplished. There is a difference between assertiveness and arrogance.

Questions:

Are you able to spend time by yourself?

Can you receive love when given?

What are some blocks you may have to overcome?

How to Face Fear & Move Beyond It

As human beings we get caught up in fear in our lives, which can often times cause paralysis. Two phrases come to mind that are often said about fear. That it is: False Evidence Appearing Real, and that you can Face Everything and Run. There are many other acronyms for FEAR. Those were just two that popped in as I am writing this.

I have struggled with fear a lot in my own life. When I start to do really well, I get scared, fear comes up, and I sabotage myself. I know other people reading this have also done this. I think it is important to remember that fear is a guide; it involves making a choice. If you are walking down a dark alley and start to feel fear, that is helpful; it is a protective factor and can help you from getting hurt. However, as humans, many of us get paralyzed when we feel fear, and that is not what it was designed to do. Fear can increase the fight-flight, freeze, or fawn reactions in our bodies. How do you want to react? To determine this, it is important to ask yourself some questions.

Sometimes, checking in with ourselves is important. Do this by tuning into the internal dialogue that is happening. One of the best ways I ever heard was to imagine there was a mini-you following you around 24 hours a day, just saying back to you out loud all the things you are thinking in your head. How would that feel? What emotions would come up? I know for me, after about 10 minutes, I would be like, get the duct tape. Yet, we think it is okay to allow all these thoughts to continue in our heads.

One of the things I used to talk about all the time as a therapist was the difference between pain and suffering. Pain is real, it is something we feel. Suffering is caused by us. By the thoughts and situations we create around the pain. Think about that for a moment.

As a therapist, I worked mostly with eating disorders, trauma, and addictions. I heard horrific things that people experienced, and yet I was always compassionate because that was important. Sometimes, just holding space for people allows them to realize and let go. Sometimes, we get so busy in conversations with people thinking about what we are going to say next that we are not truly listening. We all need to be seen and heard. We all need witnesses in our lives to help us on our path.

It is so interesting to me that I have not been a practicing therapist for the last three years with clients, and yet I feel like I am still a therapist. When I was younger, everyone told me I was going to grow up and become a therapist. I always laughed at them, telling them they were ridiculous.

However, what is a therapist really? My definition of a therapist is someone who is compassionate and can help guide you to be healed and whole, learn life skills, and thrive in your life. So, if I go by that definition, I am proud to be a therapist.

It just seems to me there are so many people struggling in the world right now, and all need compassion, nurturing, and guidance. How do we help each other? How do we provide guidance? Does it matter what you call yourself? That is just a title, and titles do not matter; your actions and how you interact are what matters. I kept trying to get away from being called a therapist, but it is so much a part of my nature that maybe it is time for me to accept that label and realize I am here to guide, enlighten, and provide paths for people. Sometimes, it is important to just be who you really are, no matter what it is called, because being true to yourself is what really counts. In the end, after you take your last breath or have a near-death experience, it is your soul's life review, not anyone elses. What do you want to leave behind? How do you want to be seen? These are some interesting questions to think about.

Questions:

What is the worst thing that can happen if I move forward with whatever is causing me to feel fear?

What am I afraid of?

Am I afraid of succeeding?

Am I afraid of failure?

What causes me to have fear when I think about reaching my true heart's desire?

Technology

I was talking to a friend of mine about cell phones. I have talked about this in a lot of podcasts and may have mentioned it in one of my other books. However, it bears repeating. When we are on our cell phones, the signal is beamed to a cell tower and then beamed back. Now think about how many people are making angry phone calls, screaming, yelling, etc. All that energy is being beamed back to us. Wonder why we can never get out of negative cycles? I believe this is part of the reason.

When I was growing up, we had rotatory phones and then touch-tone phones. Yes, I am old, and technology is developing very quickly. With that said, we need to develop human consciousness with technology because if we lose our hearts and the ability to connect to our surroundings, technology will win and take humanity over.

Back to rotatory and touch-tone phones, the ones with the wires, not the portable touch-tone phones. When you were mad, there was nothing as satisfying as the sound of slamming the phone down. Now, we just press a button. Where do all those feelings and emotions go that we used to take out on the phone? The act of slamming the phone down actually released some of the feeling. Pressing the end button just doesn't do it.

Technology has changed so quickly in my lifetime. I remember learning how to type on a typewriter with no letters and numbers on the keys so you had to remember where the keys were. I remember when you called someone and you got a busy signal it did not go to voice mail.

One of the other things I like to talk about is call waiting. I have talked about this many times before. I used to use this as an example when I was running therapy groups. When you are on the phone and another call comes in, often, people take the other call and either hang up on you or ask you to hold. What does that do to the person's self-esteem? Depending on how you feel about yourself, it may greatly affect you as you are now not good enough to continue to talk to the person. The other call was more important than you. Just think about that subtle message for a few minutes.

These are not things we stop and think about, and yet, they are things that greatly affect us. Just take social media as whole, there are positives and negatives. How you chose to use it and how it affects your life are up to you. We are losing ourselves and our connection to ourselves due to all this technology and forgetting how to connect within.

Growing up I had to learn how to read paper maps, measure the distance, and write down the directions or navigate in the car while someone else was driving. Now we just plug addresses in and are given multiple ways of getting somewhere. We are losing our ability to think, to intuit, to trust ourselves.

In my reawakening I was fortunate enough to be taken to the lab in Atlantis where things were created. I got to play with all the technology and see how it worked. Sometimes I still go there in a meditation, but not as often.

I am often taken to Egypt in meditations and shown ancient healing methods, places, and how energy and technology were blended together. How the pyramids were built with sound and vibration and the connection to nature we used to have.

Questions:

How does technology affect you?

How do you feel after looking through social media and seeing what other people are doing?

How do you feel if you are the person being asked to wait while the person you were talking to takes another call?

Section Three:

Meditations

Adrenal Thyroid Meditation

Imagine you are in a serene, sacred healing place designed just for you. Whatever pops into your mind gives you a sense of peace and calm. Take some deep breaths in and out and let the calmness and quiet wash over and through you.

In the distance, you see a pagoda, and you walk towards it. As you approach, you start to feel an even greater sense of calm and peace. Inside the pagoda, you notice a massage table made of a beautiful blue crystal. You are being called to lie down on the table. Even though it is made of crystal, you find it very comfortable. You feel yourself sinking in, feeling more peaceful than you could imagine. You notice your body, soul, and Spirit start to relax with each breath, and you feel more tranquil.

You drift into a deep state of relaxation and feel cool blue lights above and below each chakra, calming, soothing, and putting your body back into harmony and balance.

Allow yourself to fully take in this healing you are receiving and know you can take this feeling with you when you leave.

Your body is now aligned with peace, quiet and a new sense of calm. There is no need for your body and immune system to be on hyper alert anymore. You are safe, whole and healed. Believe it, breathe it in, and be it.

From this relaxed, centered, and peaceful state, you send a message from your higher self to your physical body for all systems in your body to work together in perfect balance, harmony and order.

When you are ready, get up from the crystal massage table, walk back through your sacred space, and come back to the present time and space. Open your eyes feeling refreshed, healed, whole and balanced.

Questions:

What did your pagoda feel like?

What kind of blue crystal was your massage table?

Did you feel more relaxed at the end of the meditation?

What came up for you?

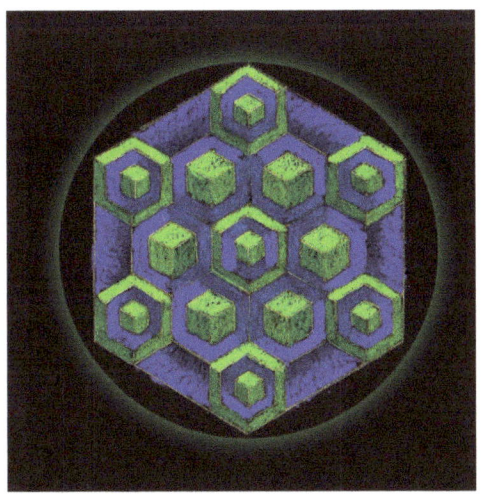

Rainbow Flame Meditation

Get comfortable in your seated position. Close your eyes, take a couple of deep breaths in and out. Now imagine you are in whatever outdoor space feels peaceful, calm and inviting to you. It could be the beach, the mountains, a meadow, a garden, etc. Take a moment to get comfortable in your outdoor space. As you are walking around taking in the sights, sounds, and smells, you see a bench in the distance. Start to walk toward the bench.

As you reach the emerald, green and gold bench you sit down and your issues, stresses, and fears drift away. You start to feel relaxed, calm and peaceful.

As you are sitting on your bench, a rainbow flame forms about six inches in front of you. It is the most brilliant burning rainbow light you have ever seen. You feel a deep sense of peace.

As you take a deep breath, you start to see, sense, or feel a smaller rainbow break off from the one in front of you and merge with your root or first chakra at the base of your spine. As the rainbow flame locks into your root chakra, it burns away any survival issues you hold inside you. Fears about being yourself fully in the world, your insecurities of being in your full power, fully opening your heart, using your voice to the fullest, trusting your intuition, and your connection to everything on the survival level. It is important to remember and know each chakra has seven layers.

You take another deep breath, and part of the rainbow flame in front of you separates and merges with your second or sacral chakra. This is the sacral or second chakra and is about being who you are meant to be out in the world. It burns away any survival issues, any fears about being yourself fully in the world, your insecurities of being in your full power, fully opening your heart, using your voice to the fullest, trusting your intuition, and connection to everything that is on the second chakra level.

You take another deep breath, and part of the rainbow flame separates and merges with your third chakra, your solar plexus or power chakra. It burns away any survival issues, any fears about being yourself fully in the world, your insecurities of being in your full power, fully opening your heart, using your voice to the fullest, trusting your intuition, and connection to everything that is on the power chakra level

You take another deep breath, and part of the rainbow flame separates and merges with your heart chakra. The fourth chakra. This chakra helps you fully live from a heart space and be open to receiving and sending love. It burns away any survival issues, fears about being yourself fully in the world, your insecurities of being in your full power, fully opening your heart, using your voice to the fullest, trusting your intuition, and connection to everything on the heart chakra level.

You take another deep breath; part of the rainbow flame separates and merges with your throat chakra. This chakra helps you use your voice, your creativity, and your point of view. It burns away any survival issues, any fears about being yourself fully in the world, your insecurities about being in your full power, fully opening your heart, using your voice to the fullest, trusting your intuition, and connecting to everything on the Throat chakra level.

You take another deep breath, and part of the rainbow flame separates and merges with your third eye chakra. This chakra is all about your intuition, seeing, hearing, knowing, and all the Clair senses. It burns away any survival issues, fears about being yourself fully in the world, insecurities about being in your full power, fully opening your heart, using your voice to the fullest, trusting your intuition, and connecting to everything that is on the third eye chakra level.

Lastly, take one more deep breath in, and part of the rainbow flame separates and merges with your crown chakra. It is time to reconnect to all that is and trust your connection. It burns away any survival issues, fears about being yourself fully in the world, and insecurities about being in your full power, fully opening your heart, using your voice to the fullest, trusting your intuition, and connecting to everything on the crown chakra level.

All the flames are burning brightly in your chakras, and your body has become the rainbow light. You are balanced, cleared, cleansed, healed, and harmonized with all your frequencies. The rainbow light connects you to the light within yourself, the Earth, and the cosmos.

Please take a moment and see how it feels to have all your chakras aligned, lit up, and let go of residue thoughts that no longer serve you. The rainbow light reforms, taking a small part of the flame from each of your chakras. The rainbow flame forms a bubble around your energy field so you can learn, explore, and feel safe.

It is now time to start coming back. Please stand up from the bench. Allow yourself to get your bearings, then walk back through the outdoor space you created and return to your room. Wiggle your fingers and toes and fully allow yourself to come back.

Questions:

What did you notice when the rainbow flame was placed in each chakra?

Were there any chakras that were more difficult or harder to put the rainbow flame in?

How did you feel once you were attuned to the rainbow flame?

Did you feel peaceful during the meditation?

Healing Pyramid Meditation

Sit or lie down, whatever is comfortable for you. Take some deep breaths in and out. Allow your mind to relax and center yourself. Just focus on breathing in and out.

I want you to imagine an outdoor space, whatever outdoor space you are called to or gives you a sense of comfort. It could be a garden, a beach, a lake, a meadow, mountains, etc. Walk around in the outdoor space you created. Notice if anyone else is there with you, any animals, vegetation, flowers, or trees. What stands out to you in the landscape you are visiting? Just allow whatever flows into your mind and senses. Notice if any feelings are coming up for you.

In the distance, you see a pyramid at least three stories or more. The pyramid can be any color you imagine it to be. You start to feel called to walk towards your pyramid. You feel a sense of wonder, excitement, and hope. As you reach the pyramid, you find the door is open for you, and you enter your pyramid. You walk towards the middle of the pyramid, and you know this is the middle because a mandala is embedded in the ground. The mandala is the exact color or colors and shape you need. As you stand in the mandala's center, white and golden light surrounds you, and you feel yourself gently being lifted and floating toward the middle of the pyramid. You stop once you reach the middle of the pyramid and feel safe. The beam of light will hold you in place.

You find yourself drawn to looking up to the top or apex of the pyramid where you see rainbow lights and strands of DNA wrapping around the white and golden tube of light you are being suspended and held in. As the rainbow lights and DNA strands come down, you slowly start to rotate. You know that this energy, light, and DNA are coming down just for you to bring you into optimal alignment for your health and well-being.

What colors are you sensing, feeling, seeing, or knowing? Can you sense your DNA swirling around you, making adjustments? You allow yourself to open and fully receive this healing and the knowledge being encoded in you. You start to notice that you have stopped rotating and are slowly descending back to the mandala's center on the floor. You feel aligned, energized, healed, and whole.

You exit your personal pyramid and are back in your outdoor space, connecting with nature and breathing in the air. You notice that everything feels a little crisper, the smells are more potent, and you feel more connected and alive. You now return to your sitting or lying position, taking a couple of deep breaths in and out and wiggling your toes and fingers to bring yourself back fully into the room you started from.

Questions:

What was this like for you?

What messages did you get?

Did you see, feel, or notice what was swirling around you when you were suspended?

What did it feel like to be suspended and healed?

Are you willing to keep this new frequency and vibration and continue to grow into it?

Epilogue

Thank you for taking this journey with us. We hope we have illuminated some issues, provided guidance and wisdom, and left you with hope and trust.

We wish you a renewed sense of faith that anything is possible and that you can create the reality you choose.

We wish for you to feel safe, to be the most authentic version of yourself, and to put that out into the world.

Only love is real; everything else is an illusion.

Go in peace, go in love, and create from this space of joy.

—The Collective

About the Author

Gail Alexander, No-Nonsense Intuitive, Life Coach, Author, Speaker, Medium, Therapist, and Multidimensional Artist

How often have you heard, "The truth is out there." Or "If you want answers, look within." And how many times did you respond that you didn't have the first clue what to do with statements like that?

That's where Gail Alexander comes in. She actually does know. Gail knows how to access information that you haven't learned to find for yourself.

Gail has since studied many different healing traditions, including ARCH (Ancient Rainbow Conscious Healing), Angelic Healing Fire, DNA Theta Healing, EFT, Reiki, and Quantum Touch. Intuitively, she assesses which to use with each client and may draw on and interweave aspects of each.

She is becoming especially well-known for the extraordinarily beautiful, energy-infused mandalas she channels.

One day we will all step into our ability to access the energy around us. Until then, whether it's physical, mental, emotional or spiritual healing, questions about those who have transitioned, or if something is out of balance in your life, Gail Alexander is honored to be of service to you and others looking for answers they feel are just out of their reach.

www.Gail-Alexander.com

https://linktr.ee/GailAlexander

Other Books by Gail Alexander

Mandalas Created for the World & Humanity

Energy Mandalas of Crystals & Stones

Healing Energies Mandala Coloring Book

I Don't Know How I Know . . . I Just Know

I Still Know What I Know

Sharing What I Know

Jesus and the Jewish Girl

Be Free to Be Yourself: The Magical Unicorn

The Great Awakening of 2020: A Mandalic Journey

Mandala Coloring Book: Healing Edition

Mandala Coloring Book: Dolphin, Unicorn and
Mermaid Edition

Mandala Coloring Book: Winged Being Edition

www.ingramcontent.com/pod-product-compliance
Lightning Source LLC
Chambersburg PA
CBHW051223120626
46547CB00013B/1477